ROBi FOR THE CLOSE FRiENDS

ALAiN AUDERSET

WESTBOW
PRESS
A DIVISION OF THOMAS NELSON

WestBow Press books may be ordered through booksellers or by contacting:

WestBow Press
A Division of Thomas Nelson
1663 Liberty Drive
Bloomington, IN 47403
www.westbowpress.com
1-(866) 928-1240

Because of the dynamic nature of the Internet, any web addresses or links contained in this book may have changed since publication and may no longer be valid. The views expressed in this work are solely those of the author and do not necessarily reflect the views of the publisher, and the publisher hereby disclaims any responsibility for them.

Any people depicted in stock imagery provided by Thinkstock are models, and such images are being used for illustrative purposes only.

Certain stock imagery © Thinkstock.

ISBN: 978-1-4497-1916-6 (sc)
ISBN: 978-1-4497-1917-3 (e)

Library of Congress Control Number: 2011931401

Printed in the United States of America

WestBow Press rev. date: 09/21/2011

To Lilou,
Séphora, Silas, Océane-Aimée,
and Benjamin-Aimé...
whom I love so much...

THANKS

to David von Gunten, the genious who created this very particular font (so similar to the writing of the author) and adapted the text in the balloons, to Christelle Reboulet for the calligraphy (www.calligraphie.fr) used when the Creator speaks, to Philippe Siraut who succeeded in coordinating all the administrative tasks, to Kathryne Landry, Helen Steiger and Laurent Bachmann for the numerous corrections, to... David van der Maas, Raphael Poggioni, Jonathan Bigler, Sarah Cox, Nicolas Ziegert, Déborah Carpentier, Sara-Anna Clement, Keren Boinay, G. Pestalozzi, Noel Purdy, Julie Wooden and to all the ones whom I have forgotten (once again) and who have taken part from near or far to the adaptation of this comic book in English and, in first place, thanks to Jesus-Christ who loves you so much...

1ST FLOOR
A SERIAL NUMBER?

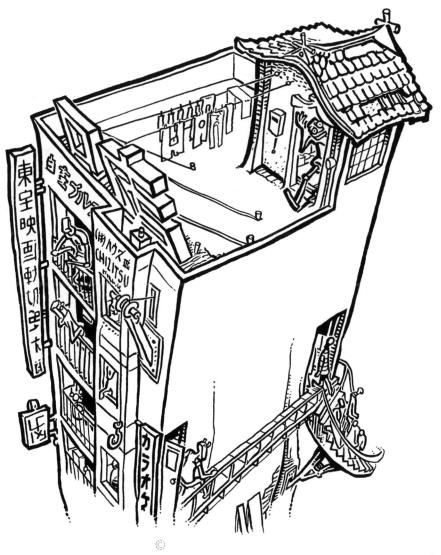

(1st ed. in French : november 2005)

www.auderset.com atelier@auderset.com Atelier Auderset, Rue de la Malathe 14, CH-2610 St-Imier, Switzerland Tél : (+41) 32 941 15 19 Fax : (+41) 32 941 37 19

Printed in the USA

Nokyo, 38'801'225,3 inhabitants.
So many people... so many small working lives... are we insignificant.?.
Are we no more than just numbers ?!
Just good enough to run the system of a society based on profit,
materialism, love of money...
Have we just become like robots !!?

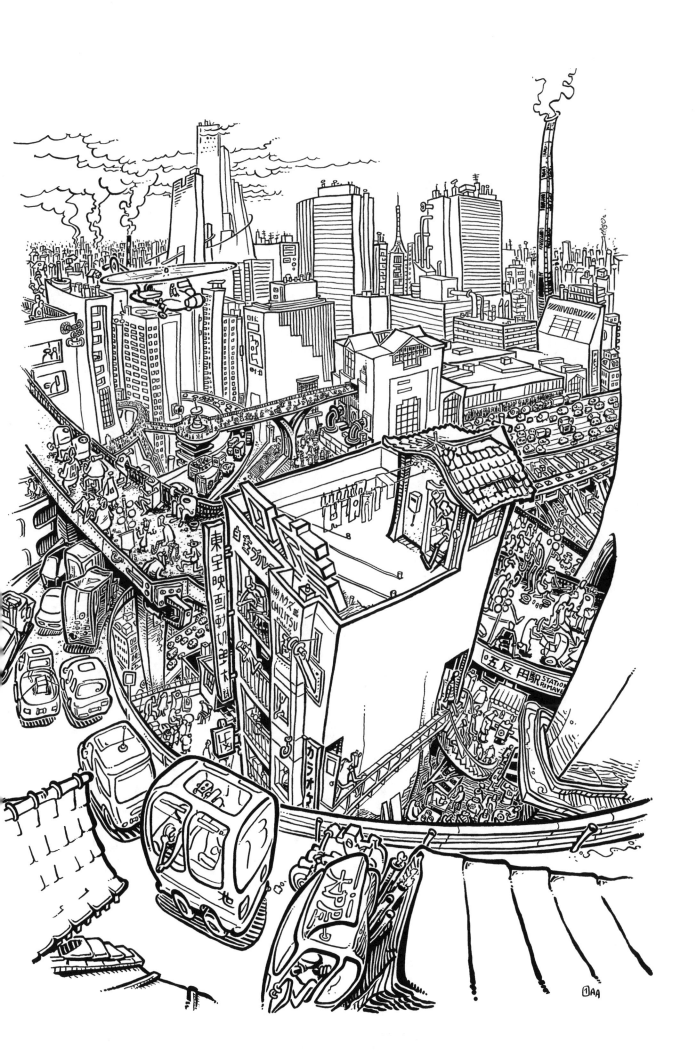

WHY DON'T WE PICK OUT OF THIS "HUMAN" MASS, ONE OF ITS NUMBER.
MOVE IN CLOSE TO HIM AND OBSERVE HIM A WHILE...
WE MAY GET SOME ANSWERS THAT CAN HELP US...(?!)

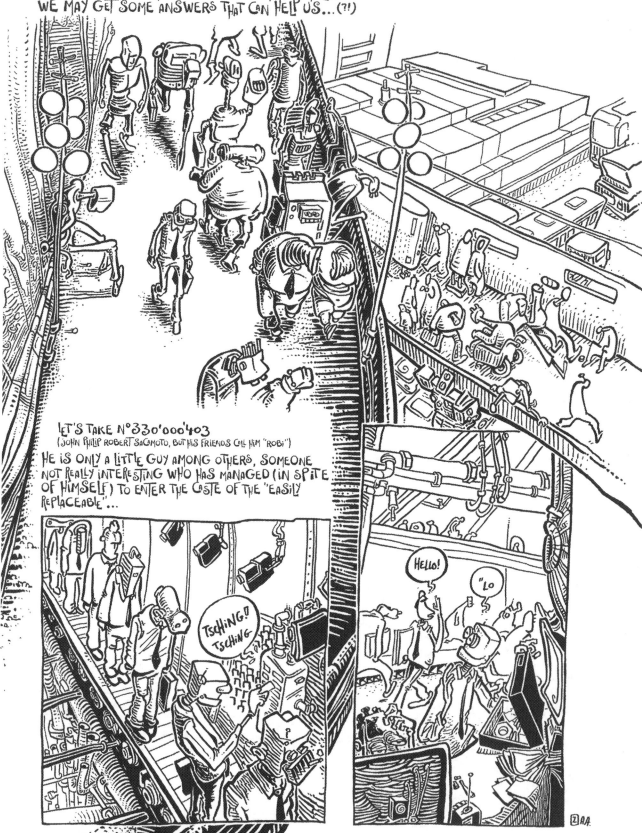

LET'S TAKE N°330'000'403
(JOHN PHILIP ROBERT SACAMOTO, BUT HIS FRIENDS CALL HIM "ROBI")
HE IS ONLY A LITTLE GUY AMONG OTHERS, SOMEONE
NOT REALLY INTERESTING WHO HAS MANAGED (IN SPITE
OF HIMSELF) TO ENTER THE CASTE OF THE "EASILY
REPLACEABLE"...

ROBi LIVED IN A WORLD HE FOUND BORING.
ALTHOUGH HE HAD A GOOD SITUATION IN A FACTORY MAKING
ALL SORTS OF USEFUL MACHINES...

THIS IS THE CANTEEN...

...AND (AS ALWAYS) WHEN COMING BACK FROM WORK,
"BAGOFLEAS" (HIS FAITHFUL COMPANION) WAS THERE, TO
WELCOME HIM JOYFULLY...

ROBI WAS SUFFERING FROM AN EMPTINESS WITHIN...

...HE WAS A PAST MASTER IN THE ART OF KEEPING UP APPEARANCES...

BUT THIS GAME NEEDED TO END...

IT'S GONNA CHANGE!!

2ND FLOOR
A GOOD DEAL

FIRST THERE WAS THE "IMAGE BOX"...

BUT UNFORTUNATELY ALL OF THESE IMAGES WERE EMPTY AND SUPERFICIAL, A SORT OF OPTIC ILLUSION...

...SO HE DECIDED TO BUY AN ORGANISED SOUND MACHINE

...HOWEVER, IT WAS ALL WELL AND GOOD TURNING UP THE SOUND TO THE MAXIMUM...

...THE SOUNDS WERE NOTHING MORE THAN "FILLINGS" OF EMOTIONS. THEY CREATED NOTHING BUT A PASSING ECHO...

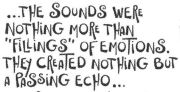

HE ALSO TRIED ALL KINDS OF OBJECTS THAT SHOULD HAVE BEEN SATISFYING, EVEN MORE SO CONSIDERING WHAT THEY WERE: THE LATEST HIT, HIGHLY TECHNICAL OR GOLD PLATED IN EXTREME... THE GOLDEN TOOTHBRUSH, RADIO-CONTROLLED MEAL...

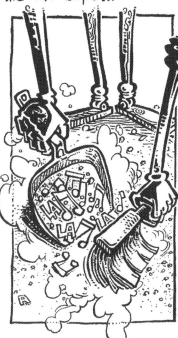

HUH ?! WHAT ARE THEY SAYING !?

WHAT !!?

...WELL OK, HOW ABOUT TURNING @%#!! THE PAGE HERE ?!

A BRAND NEW CARTOON FRAME AT SUCH A PRICE- I JUST COULDN'T RESIST!

12 A.A

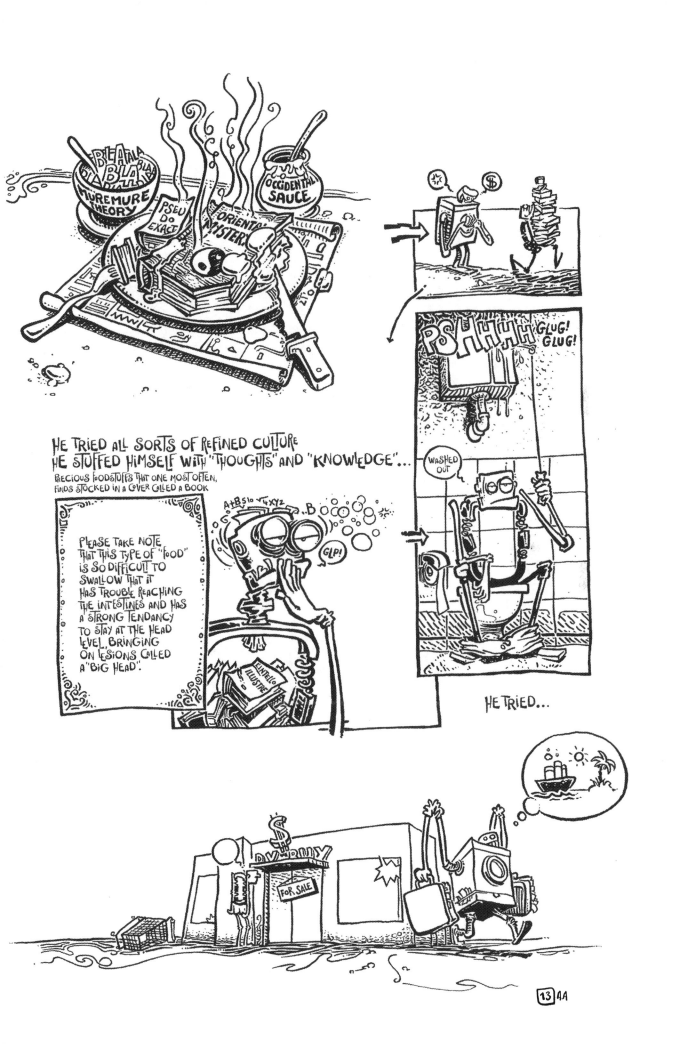

HE TRIED ALL SORTS OF REFINED CULTURE
HE STUFFED HIMSELF WITH "THOUGHTS" AND "KNOWLEDGE"...
PRECIOUS FOODSTUFFS THAT ONE MOST OFTEN
FINDS STOCKED IN A COVER CALLED A BOOK

PLEASE TAKE NOTE
THAT THIS TYPE OF "FOOD"
IS SO DIFFICULT TO
SWALLOW THAT IT
HAS TROUBLE REACHING
THE INTESTINES AND HAS
A STRONG TENDANCY
TO STAY AT THE HEAD
LEVEL, BRINGING
ON LESIONS CALLED
A "BIG HEAD".

WASHED OUT

HE TRIED...

3RD FLOOR
AN INTERESTING
PATHOLOGY

HE THEN DECIDED TO CONSULT ALL SORTS OT "SPECIALISTS"

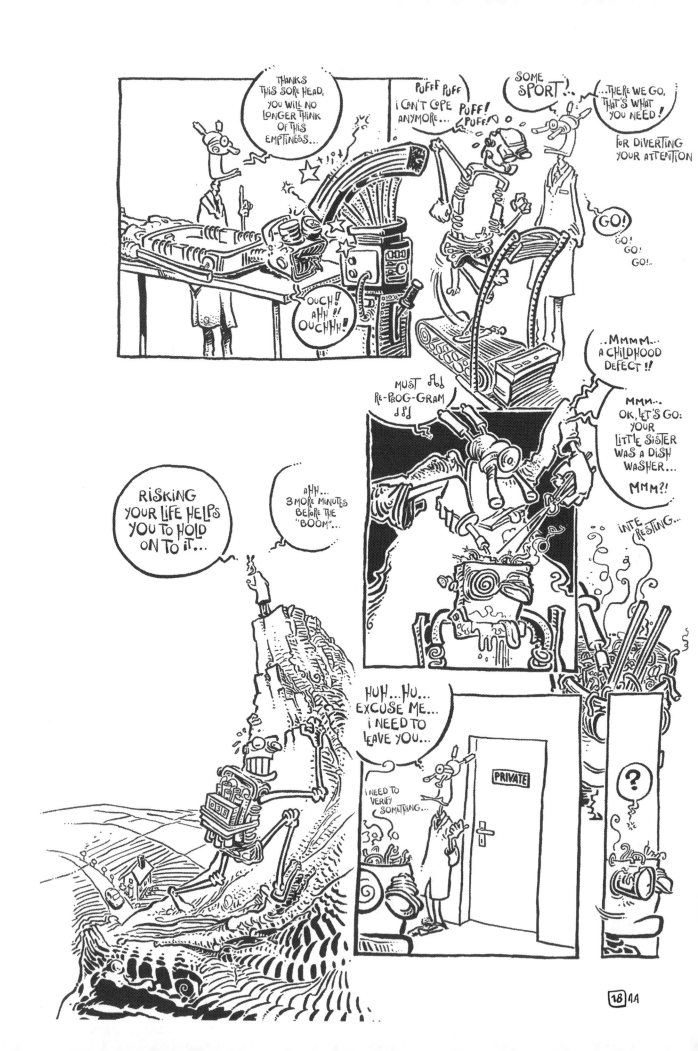

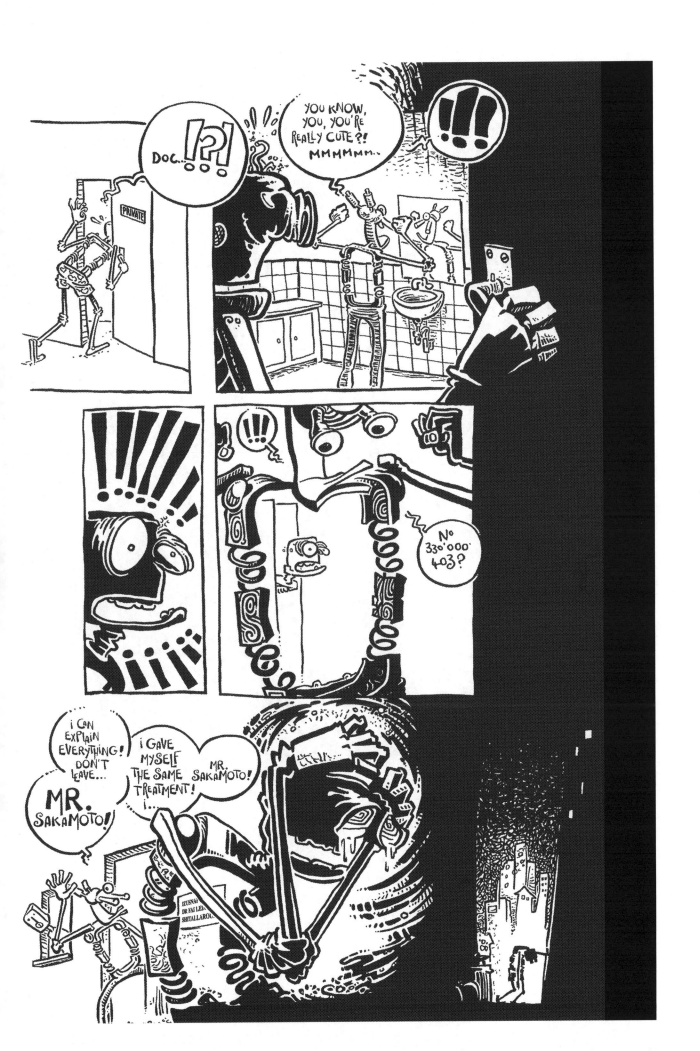

CONTRACT
BY THE PRESENT
CONTRACT, I RELINQUISH THE BURDEN OF MATERIALISM TO THE COMMUNITY OF HIS HAPPINESS "ATISHOOBLESSUTA-SUKE". ALL LEGAL RECOURSE IS EXCLUDED AND I RELIEVE THE COURT OF ALL RESPONSIBILITY WITH REGARD MY HEALTH. CONNED THE... ...AT...

(SHHH!)

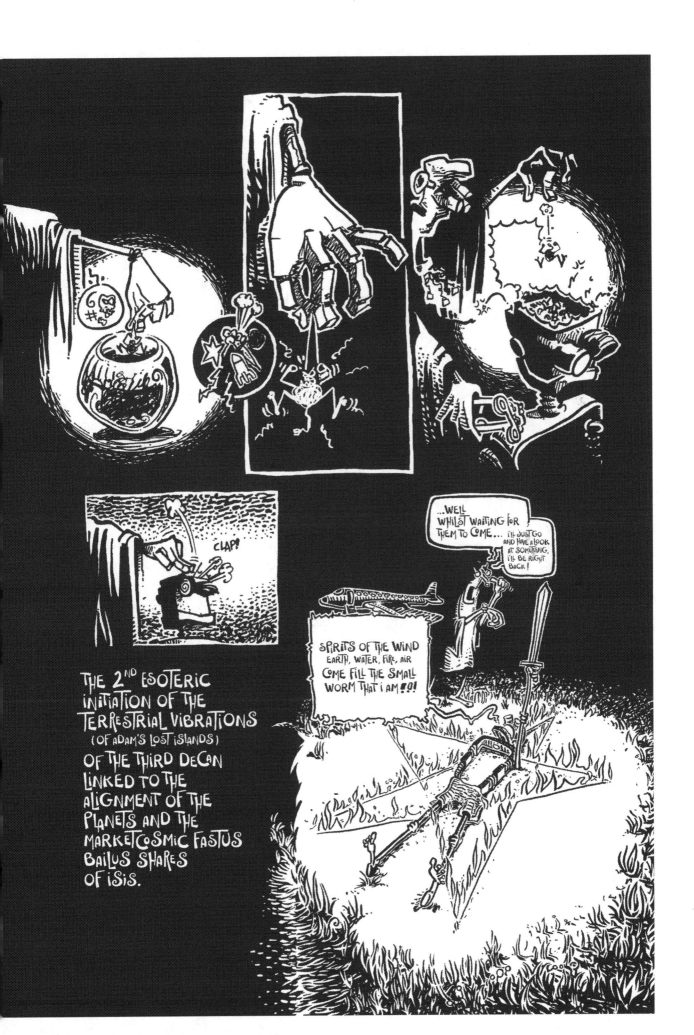

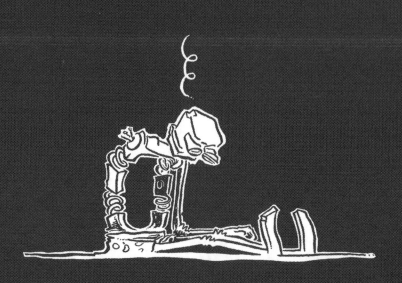

5TH FLOOR
PURSUING AN
INCLINATION

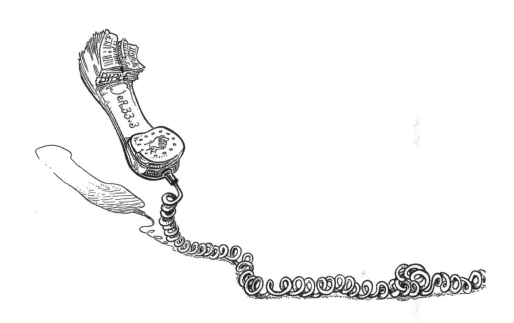

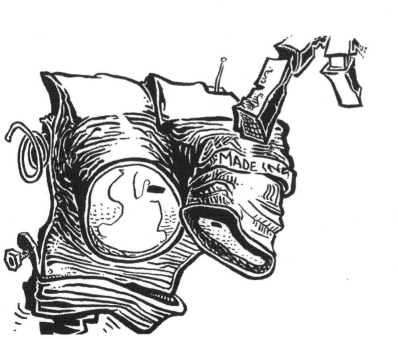

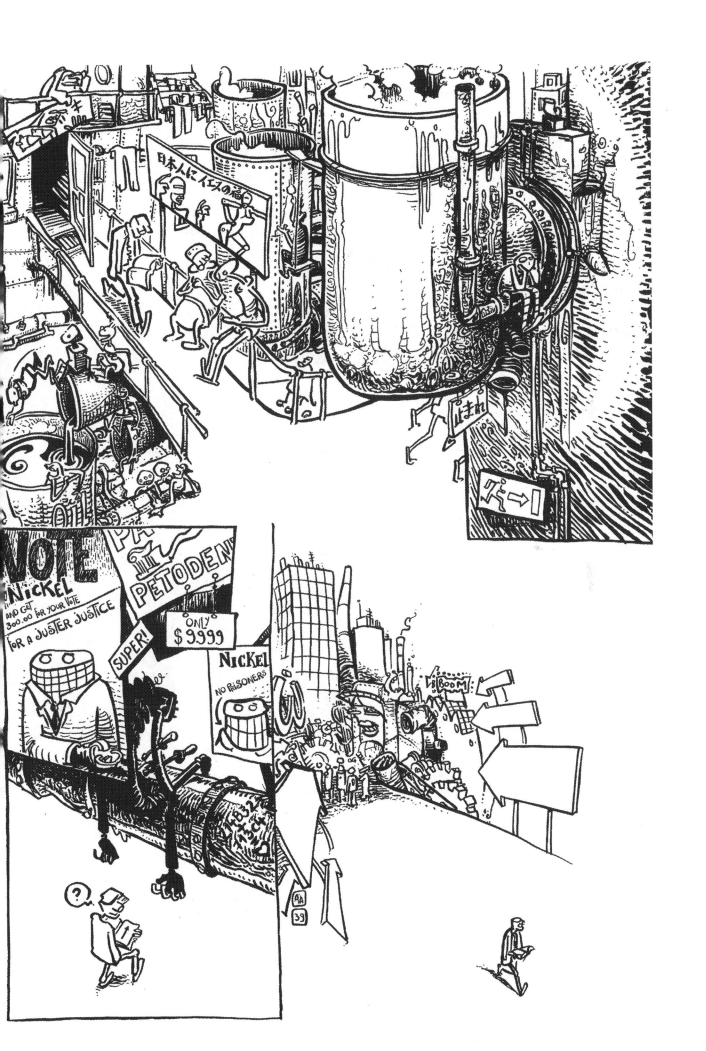

IT'S JUST BEFORE DAWN ... THAT THE NIGHT... ...IS AT ITS DARKEST AND OLDEST

A.A

ROBI
6TH FLOOR
THE MEETING POINT!

this way Robi

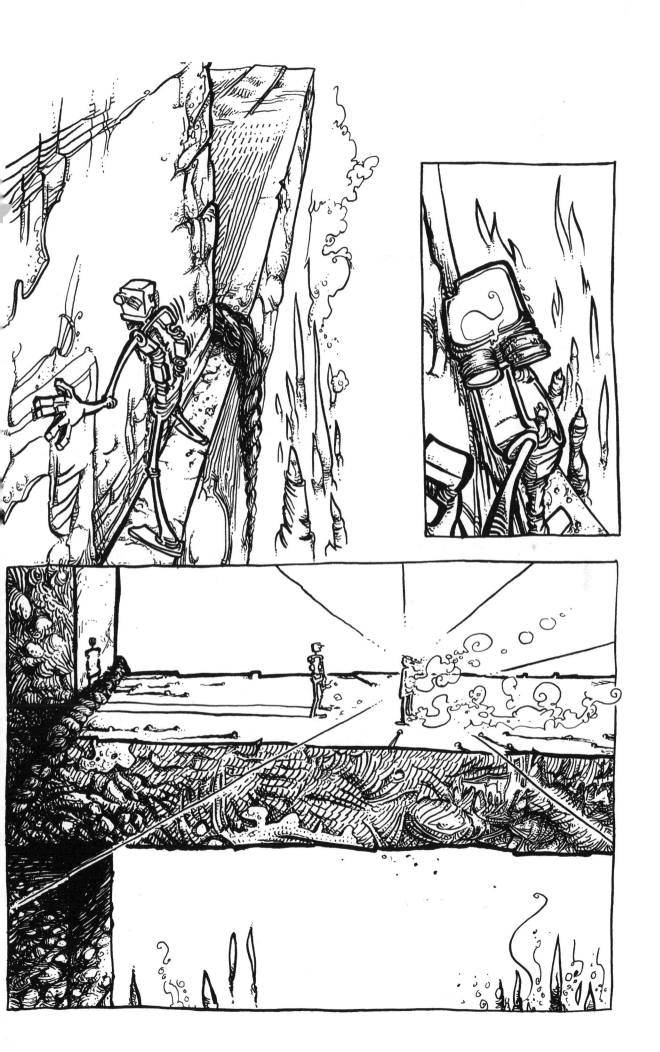

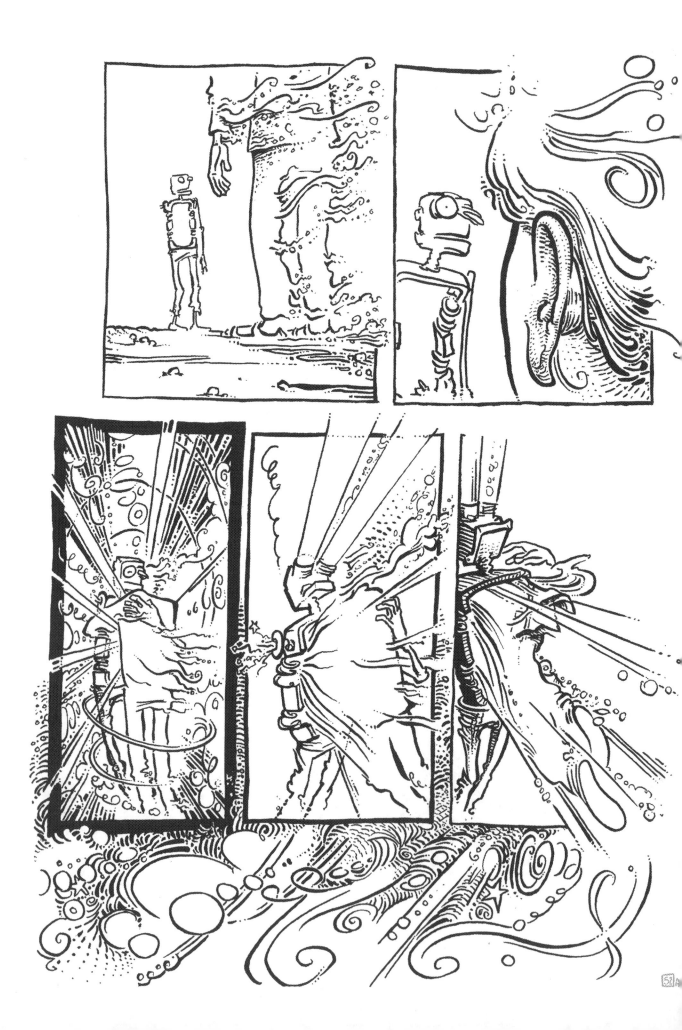

RoBi

7TH FLOOR
THE CREATOR'S HOUSE

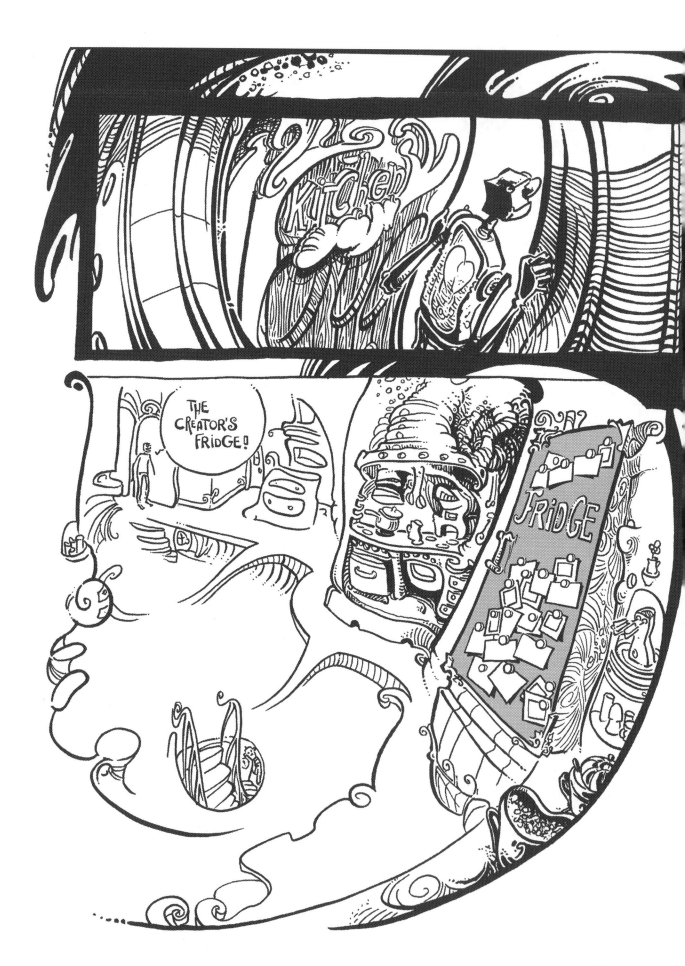

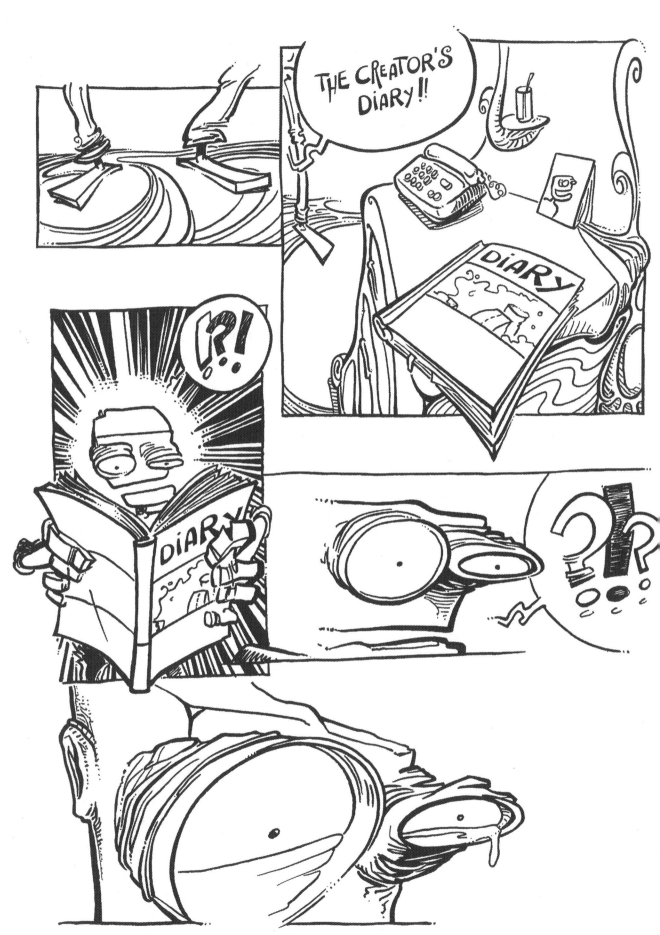

Robi
You are neither
an accident
nor the
product of
chance
Nor a number

Before I even
created you
I ardently
desired your
Existence,
I loved you
I've always loved
you
& I will love
you forever

. Every person
is a unique creation
everyone in
particular has
all my attention...
I have this
tenderness just
for you.

yes
just
for
you

You

...IN EVERY MAN'S HEART, THERE IS A "HOLE" IN THE SHAPE OF GOD...

...IN EVERY MAN'S HEART, THERE IS A "HOLE" IN THE SHAPE OF GOD...

IF ANYONE IS IN CHRIST, HE IS A NEW CREATION. THE OLD HAS GONE, THE NEW HAS COME. 2 COR 5:17...

I've never stopped loving you...

That's what the Creator is saying in the Bible (Jer. 31:3)

You 💛

CONVENTIONAL WISDOM A.AUDERSET

**From
the same
author:**

In English

In French

More info: www.auderset.com